TEEN GUIDE TO DRAWING MANGA

DRAWING
MANGA MECHA,
WEAPONS, AND
WHEELS

ANNA SOUTHGATE AND YISHAN LI

rosen publishing's
rosen central

NEW YORK

This edition published in 2013 by:

The Rosen Publishing Group, Inc.
29 East 21st Street
New York, NY 10010

Additional end matter copyright © 2013 by The Rosen Publishing Group, Inc.

Library of Congress Cataloging-in-Publication Data

Southgate, Anna.
Drawing manga mecha, weapons, and wheels/Anna Southgate, Yishan Li.—First [edition].
        pages cm.—(Teen guide to drawing manga)
Includes bibliographical references and index.
ISBN 978-1-4488-9242-6 (library binding)—
ISBN 978-1-4488-9265-5 (pbk.)—
ISBN 978-1-4488-9266-2 (6-pack)
1. Comic books, strips, etc.—Japan—Technique—Juvenile literature.
2. Cartooning—Technique—Juvenile literature. I. Li, Yishan. II. Title.
NC1764.5.J3S678 2013
741.5'1—dc23

                                                                    2012034787

Manufactured in the United States of America

CPSIA Compliance Information: Batch #W13YA: For further information, contact Rosen Publishing, New York, New York, at 1-800-237-9932.

All other content copyright © 2011 Axis Books Limited, London.

CONTENTS

INTRODUCTION

Leaf through the pages of a book of manga and you are likely dazzled and amazed by the color, the textures, the dynamism, and the details. You may wonder, "How can anyone do that?" You might even wish you could draw and ink manga yourself but doubt that you could ever be as good as some of your favorite artists. The exciting truth, however, is that anyone can learn how to draw manga characters, mecha, weapons, vehicles, and other classic manga elements. And, with practice, you can become great at it.

The key is going step-by-step. Break each image down into its basic geometric shapes and sketch them down on paper. Revise and refine your lines. Add some detail and texture. Ink it with dazzling colors, deep shadows, and shiny chromatic highlights, and voilà, you are on your way to creating a manga masterpiece. This book guides you through each of these steps and serves as an expert teacher at your elbow, talking you through the process and offering just the right tips and advice at critical points. All the basics are covered, from the tools and art supplies you will need to the simplest beginning stages of sketching preliminary shapes and outlines. These basic skills are then built upon as the drawing process advances and your abilities grow. By the end, you will be mastering the high-level art

of bold and vivid coloring, dramatic shading, subtle expressiveness, convincing textures, and dynamic indications of motion.

With these new skills under your belt, you can try your hand at copying and designing variations of the many items in this book's crowded gallery of mecha, weapons, and vehicles. A wide array of humanoid, military, industrial, and medical mecha are presented to help you burnish your skills and provide inspiration for your own designs. This book also contains an impressive arsenal of weaponry, including numerous examples of swords, knives, bows and arrows, guns, grenades, cannons, missiles, rocket launchers, and light sabers. And the vehicle bays are fully loaded with awe-inspiring examples of motorbikes, jets, sports cars, buses, bullet trains, yachts, and spaceships.

Now you have the tools and supplies. You have acquired the skills. You have been introduced to the fundamental visual elements of the glittering, infinite, mysterious, and magical universe that is manga. Now there is nothing left to do but get drawing and create your own wildly imaginative and full-color world of wonder.

Chapter One
Manga Materials and Equipment

There are several ways to produce manga art. You can draw and colour images by hand, generate them on a computer or work using a combination of both. Whichever style suits you, there are plenty of options when it comes to buying materials. This section of the book outlines the basics in terms of paper, pencils, inking pens, markers and paints, and will help you to make choices that work for you.

MATERIALS AND EQUIPMENT

Artists have their preferences when it comes to equipment, but regardless of personal favourites, you will need a basic set of materials that will enable you to sketch, ink and colour your manga art. The items discussed here are only a guide – don't be afraid to experiment to find out what works best for you.

PAPERS

You will need two types of paper – one for creating sketches, the other for producing finished colour artwork.

For quickly jotting down ideas, almost any piece of scrap paper will do. For more developed sketching, though, use tracing paper. Tracing paper provides a smooth surface, helping you to sketch freely. It is also forgiving – any mistakes can easily be erased several times over. Typically, tracing paper comes in pads. Choose a pad that is around 90gsm (24lb) in weight for best results – lighter tracing papers may buckle and heavier ones are not suitable for sketching. Once you have finished sketching out ideas, you will need to transfer them to the paper you want to produce your finished coloured art on. To do this, you will have to trace over your pencil sketch, so the paper you choose cannot be too opaque or heavy – otherwise you will not be able to see the sketch underneath. Choose a paper around 60gsm (16lb) for this. The type of paper you use is also important. If you are going to colour using marker pens, use marker or layout paper. Both of these types are very good at holding the ink found in markers. Other papers of the same weight can cause the marker ink to bleed, that is, the ink soaks beyond the inked lines of your drawing and produces fuzzy edges. This does not look good. You may wish to colour your art using other materials, such as coloured pencils or watercolours. Drawing paper is good for graphite pencil and inked-only art (such as that found in the majority of manga comic books),

Experiment with different papers to find the one that suits your style of drawing and colouring best. Watercolour papers can be ideal if you like using lots of wet colour like inks to render your manga.

while heavyweight watercolour papers hold wet paint and coloured inks and come in a variety of surface textures.

Again, don't be afraid to experiment: you can buy many types of papers in single sheets while you find the ones that suit your artwork best.

PENCILS

The next step is to choose some pencils for your sketches. Pencil sketching is probably the most important stage, and always comes first when producing manga art (you cannot skip ahead to the inking stage), so make sure you choose pencils that feel good in your hand and allow you to express your ideas freely.

Pencils are manufactured in a range of hard and soft leads. Hard leads are designated by the letter H and soft leads by the letter B. Both come in six levels – 6H is the hardest lead and 6B is the softest. In the middle is HB, a halfway mark between the two ranges. Generally, an HB and a 2B lead will serve most sketching purposes, with the softer lead being especially useful for loose, idea sketches, and the harder for more final lines.

Alternatively, you can opt for mechanical pencils. Also called self-propelling pencils, these come in a variety of lead grades and widths and never lose their point, making sharpening traditional wood-cased pencils a thing of the past. Whether you use one is entirely up to you

Graphite pencils are ideal for getting your ideas down on paper, and producing your initial drawing. The pencil drawing is probably the most important stage in creating your artwork. Choose an HB and a 2B to start with.

– it is possible to get excellent results whichever model you choose.

COLOURED PENCILS

Coloured pencils are effective and versatile colouring tools. A good box of pencils contains around 100 colours and will last for a long time, since a blunt pencil just needs sharpening, not replacing or refilling. Unlike with markers, successive layers of tone and shade can be built up with the same pencil, by gradually increasing the pressure on the pencil lead.

COPIC MARKERS
WARM AND COOL GREYS

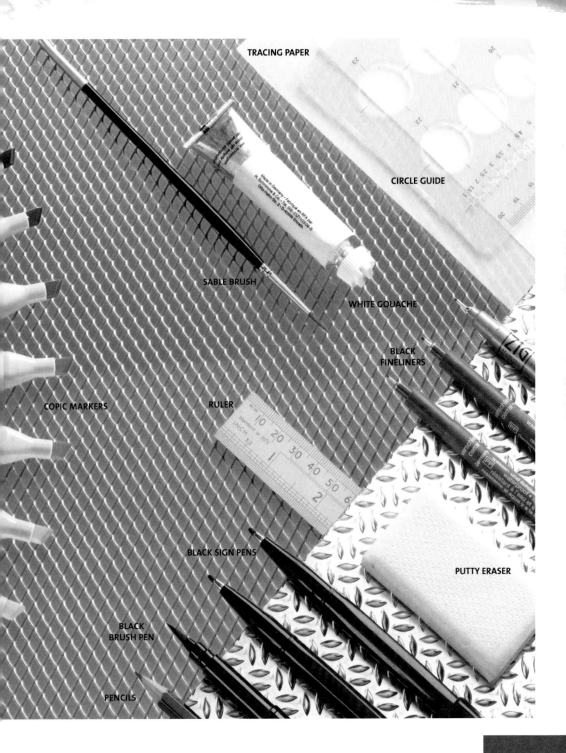

TRACING PAPER

CIRCLE GUIDE

SABLE BRUSH

WHITE GOUACHE

BLACK FINELINERS

COPIC MARKERS

RULER

BLACK SIGN PENS

PUTTY ERASER

BLACK BRUSH PEN

PENCILS

A good quality eraser or putty eraser is an essential item for removing unwanted pencil lines and for cleaning up your inked drawing before you start applying the colour.

Felt-tip pens are the ideal way to ink your sketches. A fineliner, medium-tip pen and sign pen should meet all of your needs, whatever your style and preferred subjects. A few coloured felt-tip pens can be a good addition to your kit, allowing you to introduce colour at the inking stage.

You can then build further colour by using a different colour pencil. Coloured pencils are also useful for adding detail, which is usually achieved by inking. This means that a more subtle level of detail can be achieved without having to ink in all lines. It is worth buying quality pencils. They do make a difference to the standard of your art and will not fade with age.

SHARPENERS AND ERASERS

If you use wooden pencils, you will need to get a quality sharpener; this is a small but essential piece of equipment. Electric sharpeners work very well and are also very fast; they last a long time too. Otherwise, a handheld sharpener is fine. One that comes with a couple of spare blades can be a worthwhile investment, to ensure that your pencils are always sharp. Along with a sharpener, you will need an eraser

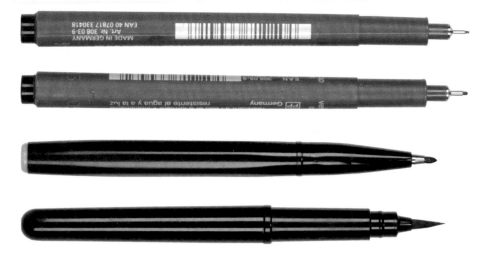

for removing any visible pencil lines from your inked sketches prior to colouring. Choose a high-quality eraser that does not smudge the pencil lead, scuff the paper, or leave dirty fragments all over your work. A soft putty eraser works best, since it absorbs pencil lead rather than just rubbing it away. For this reason, putty erasers do become dirty with use. Keep yours clean by trimming it carefully with scissors every now and then.

INKING PENS

The range of inking pens can be bewildering, but some basic rules will help you select the pens you need. Inked lines in most types of manga tend to be quite bold so buy a thin-nibbed pen, about 0.5mm, and a medium-size nib, about 0.8mm. Make sure that the ink in the pens is waterproof; this won't smudge or run. Next, you will need a medium-tip felt pen. Although you won't need to use this pen very often to ink the outlines of your characters, it is still useful for filling in small detailed areas of solid black. A Pentel pen does this job well. Last, consider a pen that can create different line widths according to the amount of pressure you put on the tip. These pens replicate brushes and allow you to create flowing lines such as those seen on hair and clothing. The Pentel brush pen does this very well, delivering a steady supply of ink to the tip from a replaceable cartridge. It is a good idea to test-drive a few pens at your art shop to see which ones suit you best. All pens should produce clean, sharp lines with a deep black pigment.

Markers come in a wide variety of colours, which allows you to achieve subtle variations in tone. In addition to a thick nib for broad areas of colour, the Copic markers shown here feature a thin nib for fine detail.

A selection of warm and cool greys is a useful addition to your marker colours and most ranges feature several different shades. These are ideal for shading on faces, hair, and clothes.

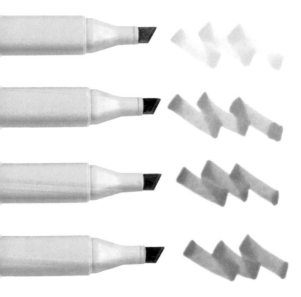

MARKERS AND COLOURING AIDS

Many artists use markers, rather than paint, to colour their artwork, because markers are easy to use and come in a huge variety of colours and shades. Good-quality markers, such as those made by Chartpak, Letraset or Copic, produce excellent, vibrant results, allowing you to build up multiple layers of colour so you can create rich, detailed work and precise areas of shading. Make sure that you use your markers with marker or layout paper to avoid bleeding. Markers are often refillable, so they last a long time. The downside is that they are expensive,

so choose a limited number of colours to start with, and add as your needs evolve. As always, test out a few markers in your art store before buying any.

However, markers are not the only colouring media. Paints and gouache also produce excellent results, and can give your work a distinctive look. Add white gouache, which comes in a tube, to your work to create highlights and sparkles of light. Apply it in small quantities with a good-quality watercolour brush. It is also possible to colour your artwork on computer. This is quick to do, although obviously there is a high initial outlay. It also tends to produce flatter colour than markers or paints.

DRAWING AIDS

Most of your sketching will be done freehand, but there are situations, especially with man-made objects such as the edges of buildings or the wheels of a car, when your line work needs to be crisp and sharp to create the right look.

If you are colouring with gouache or watercolour paint, then a selection of sizes of good quality sable watercolour brushes are invaluable.

Rulers, circle guides and compasses all provide this accuracy. Rulers are either metal or plastic; in most cases, plastic ones work best, though metal ones tend to last longer. For circles, use a circle guide, which is a plastic sheet with a wide variety of different-sized holes stamped out of it. If the circle you want to draw is too big for the circle guide, use a compass that can hold a pencil and inking pen.

If you want to draw manga comic strips, a pencil and a standard 30cm (12in) ruler are the only tools you will need to plan out your panels. (It is also possible to draw them digitally on computer.) Just remember to buy a quality ruler with an edge that will suit your pencils and pens and won't chip over time. A plastic one will generally last longer than a wooden one. Creating speech bubbles inside the panels is best done by hand, but templates are available if you need help. They do make your work look neat, they are generally cheap to buy, and they

Working freehand allows great freedom of expression and is ideal when you are working out a sketch, but you will find times when precision is necessary. Use compasses or a circle guide for circles and ellipses to keep your work sharp. Choose compasses that can be adjusted to hold both pencils and pens.

do not need replacing often. You can buy them in most art shops. It is possible to order authentic manga templates from Japan, but these are not really necessary unless you want to start collecting authentic manga art equipment. You can make your own templates out of cardboard if the ones in the shops do not suit your needs.

DRAWING BOARD

A drawing board is useful, since working on a flat table for a long time can give you a backache. Lots of different models are available, but all should be adjustable to the angle at which you want to work. They also come in a wide variety of sizes, from ones that sit on your lap or a tabletop to large work tables. If you do not want to invest in one immediately, it is possible to prop a piece of smooth, flat plywood about 60cm (24in) x 45cm (18in) on your desk. Put a small box underneath to create an angled surface.

A mannequin can be placed in different poses, helping you to visualise action and movement.

mannequin

A mannequin is an excellent tool for helping you to establish correct anatomical proportions, particularly for simpler poses such as walking and running. All the limbs are jointed to mimic human movement. They are also relatively cheap, but bear in mind that other reference materials may be necessary for more complicated movements, such as those involving martial arts. Photographic reference is often useful too.

USING A COMPUTER

When your sketches start coming easily and the more difficult features, such as texture and perspective, begin to look more convincing, you will be confident enough to expand on the range of scenes you draw. You might even begin to compose cartoon strips of your own or, at the very least, draw compositions in which several characters interact with each other – such as a battle scene.

Once you reach this stage, you might find it useful to start using a computer alongside your regular art materials. Used with a software program, like Adobe Photoshop, you can colour scanned-in sketches quickly and easily. You will also have a much wider range of colours to use, and can experiment at will. Moving one step further, a computer can save you a lot of time and energy when it comes to producing comic strips. Most software programs enable you to build a picture in layers. This means that you could have a general background layer – say a mountainous landscape – that always stays the same, plus a number of subsequent layers on

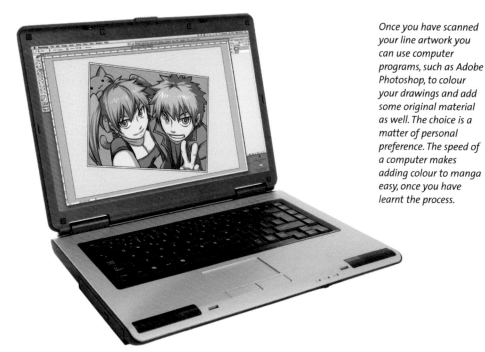

Once you have scanned your line artwork you can use computer programs, such as Adobe Photoshop, to colour your drawings and add some original material as well. The choice is a matter of personal preference. The speed of a computer makes adding colour to manga easy, once you have learnt the process.

which you can build your story. For example, you could use one layer for activity that takes place in the sky and another layer for activity that takes place on the ground. This means that you can create numerous frames simply by making changes to one layer, while leaving the others as they are. There is still a lot of work involved, but working this way does save you from having to draw the entire frame from scratch each time.

Of course, following this path means that you must invest in a computer if you don't already have one. You will also need a scanner and the relevant software. All of this can be expensive and it is worth getting your hand-drawn sketches up to a fairly accomplished level before investing too much money.

You can input a drawing straight into a computer program by using a graphics tablet and pen. The tablet plugs into your computer, much like a keyboard or mouse.

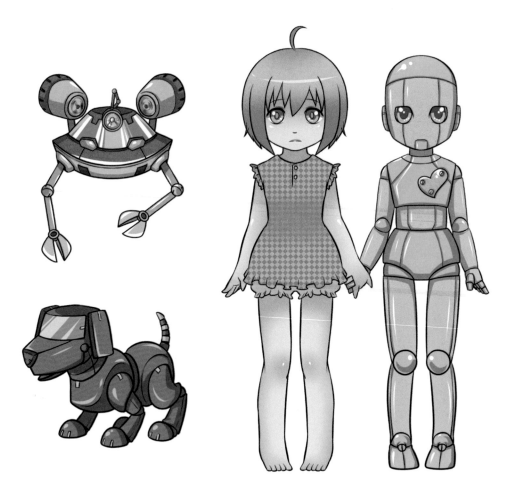

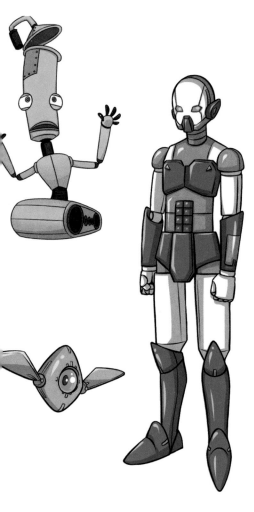

Many manga stories team mechas with the more human-looking characters. Whether based on animal or human forms, many of these creations are designed specifically for serving, fighting or performing some sort of routine, and this adds an other-worldly element to the stories. This section of the book shows you how to develop a range of mechas and offers inspiration on creating characters of your own.

FANTASY SOLDIER

There is no end of fun you can have in creating fantasy figures like this and the sci-fi bounty hunter on the following pages. This outfit combines fabrics with metal finishes. Take care in making each material look realistic.

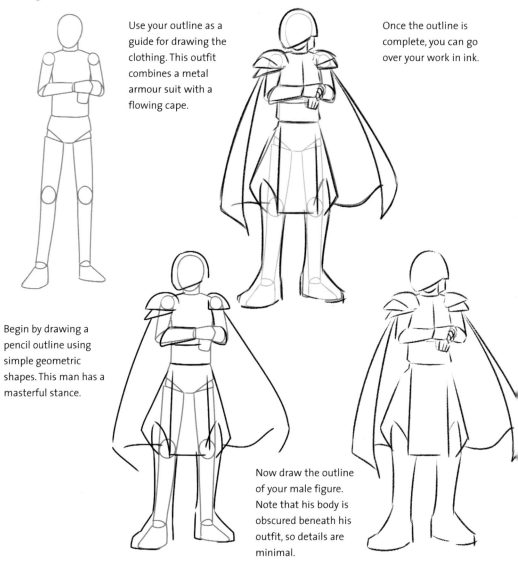

Use your outline as a guide for drawing the clothing. This outfit combines a metal armour suit with a flowing cape.

Once the outline is complete, you can go over your work in ink.

Begin by drawing a pencil outline using simple geometric shapes. This man has a masterful stance.

Now draw the outline of your male figure. Note that his body is obscured beneath his outfit, so details are minimal.

Add details, such as the armour plating of the helmet and suit. Draw in the sword and boots.

Add any final ink details, such as the decorative elements on the epaulettes, sword and boots. Give the tabard a border.

Erase your pencil lines in preparation for adding the finer ink details and colour.

Colour your work, using strong colours. Use soft shadows on the fabric areas and bright, sharp highlights on the shiny metal surfaces.

21

SCI-FI BOUNTY HUNTER

This character epitomises the departure from reality to fantasy. With no visible facial features and a curious breathing apparatus he has a menacing air about him. The toughness of his character is reflected in the hard materials used for his protective suit.

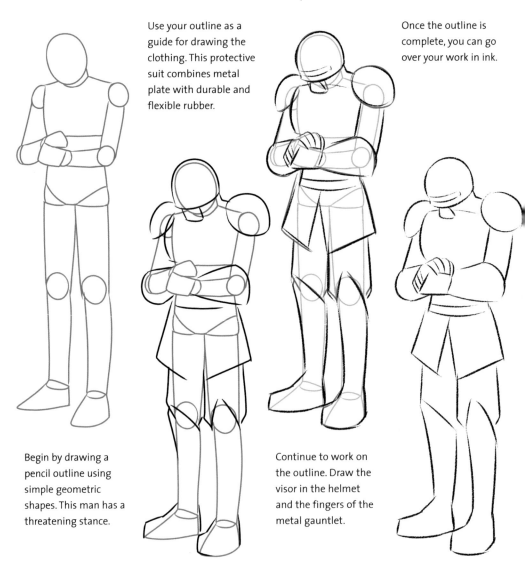

Use your outline as a guide for drawing the clothing. This protective suit combines metal plate with durable and flexible rubber.

Once the outline is complete, you can go over your work in ink.

Begin by drawing a pencil outline using simple geometric shapes. This man has a threatening stance.

Continue to work on the outline. Draw the visor in the helmet and the fingers of the metal gauntlet.

Add details, such as the armour plating of the helmet suit and the belt with all of its accessories. Draw in the tube for breathing and the boots.

Add any final ink details, such as the shading on the metal, the insignia on the armour and stiff creases in the rubber sleeves.

Erase your pencil lines in preparation for adding the finer ink details and colour.

Colour your work, using sinister colours. Use bright, sharp highlights to show how the metal surfaces catch the light.

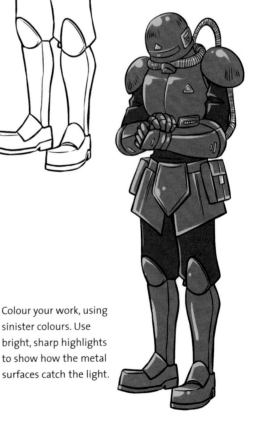

23

FAIRY GIRL

This wonderful fantasy character combines a short, fitted dress and long, stockinged legs with a full-flowing, jewel-encrusted cape. The look is light and airy, in keeping with her kindly nature. You could easily adapt the colours and hairstyle to create a malevolent version.

Begin by drawing a pencil outline using simple geometric shapes. The fairy is clutching her cape.

Now draw the outline of the dress and the fairy's figure, giving more shape to her natural curves. Draw in the hair, complete with bow, and facial features.

Use your outline as a guide for drawing the outfit – starting with the cape. Use simple lines to achieve the basic shape.

Once the outline is complete, you can go over your work in ink.

Start to work more detail into the hair. Draw the ruffled skirt of the dress. Mark the stocking tops and draw in the shoes.

Add any final ink details, such as the stitching on the bodice of the dress, and finish the jewels.

Work on the cape, adding outlines of the jewels. Finish the shoes Erase your pencil lines in preparation for adding the finer ink details and colour.

Colour your work. Use the natural curves of the body to add shadows. Work at getting the texture of the cloak's fur lining and fluffy boot trim.

TYPES OF MECHA

Many characters are based on the human form. This means that their bodies share the same proportions. This does not mean that mechas have to have human features, however.

Starting with the basic human form, it is possible to see how you can develop your manga characters into different types of mecha. Working from left to right, these examples become less recognizably human. The beauty of designing mecha characters is that there are no limits to what you can do. Many mechas are designed for specific tasks and you can have fun giving them extra limbs or other additional features that are contrived to help with that task.

A human-looking young man, well-proportioned and with recognizable features.

Though resembling the human form closely, this character is partially made from metal.

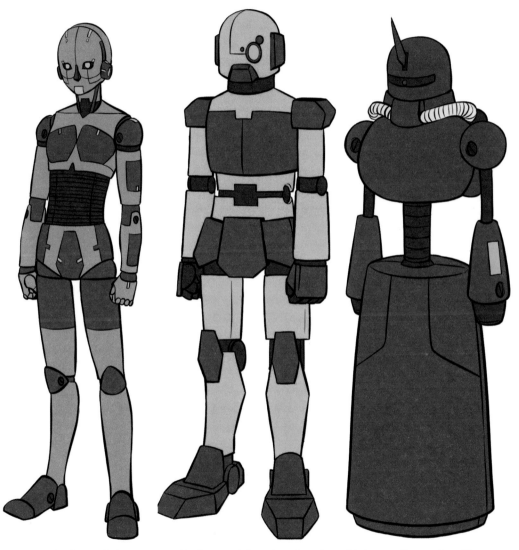

Now completely metal, the character has hinged joints and armour plate bodywork.

This character is large in scale and has a more robotic appearance with seemingly limited function.

This is a working mecha with one specific job. The features are no longer recognizably human.

DESIGN AND COMPONENTS

Mechas include anything from docile servants to big, bad fighting machines to super-strength creatures. The key to their success is being able to develop them in such a way that whatever function they have is instantly recognisable.

left A mini-housemaid. This small-scale mecha can hover in the air, making it much easier to get about a place when cleaning. The soft colours of her bodywork give her a benign appearance.

right This simple-looking mecha, has one function. With an in-built tray, she is used to fetch and carry. She moves around smoothly on casters and has basic swivel-functioning arms.

above Used for spotlighting areas, or searching out in the dark, this mecha's primary limbs have powerful in-built lights.

left This dizzy-looking character. is panicking about the latest disaster. His caterpillar-track base and flexible upper body suggest he plays a role in some sort of factory or machine works.

right A working mecha, this character has tools instead of hands at the end of his flexible arms. He is mounted on wheels for ease of mobility.

left With huge, crab-like legs, this manga scuttles about in low-level places, which suggests that his job involves some form of detection.

HUMANOID MECHA

This is one of the simplest forms of mecha, and is based on the male human body. With very similar proportions to a human, this character also shares a number of characteristics.

Use simple geometric shapes for the body parts and draw circles where all the joints should be.

With that done, you can begin to consider the mechanical aspect of your figure. Divide the body into separate moving parts, and give the shapes a more manufactured look.

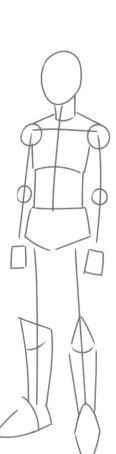

Start by drawing a very basic structure for your figure, using pencil. Try to get the proportions right – typically the head will make up one-seventh of the body, and the legs half.

Use your basic structure to draw a full outline for your figure. Keep it fairly realistic, while focusing on proportions and perspective.

Erase any unwanted pencil lines before adding the last few details in ink.

Colour up your image. Apply flat colour to start with. Consider where the light is coming from and add highlights to show where it is reflected by the mecha's armour.

Build on the detail, drawing metal plates and hinged joints. Add facial features, using them to add some character. Go over your drawing in ink.

Think about the metal element of this character and add lines to suggest seams in the armour. Add some bolts where there are joints.

31

MILITARY MECHA

Here is a mecha with a single purpose – to make war. Taking the humanoid mecha on pages 30 – 31 one step further, this military mecha has in-built weaponry. The body shape is generally more bulky with the extra, protective armour.

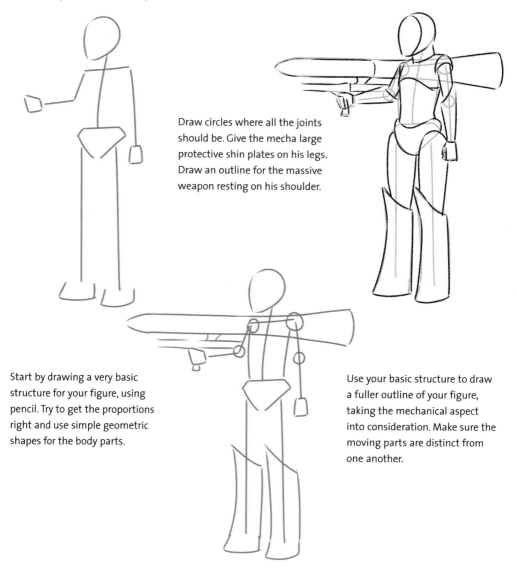

Draw circles where all the joints should be. Give the mecha large protective shin plates on his legs. Draw an outline for the massive weapon resting on his shoulder.

Start by drawing a very basic structure for your figure, using pencil. Try to get the proportions right and use simple geometric shapes for the body parts.

Use your basic structure to draw a fuller outline of your figure, taking the mechanical aspect into consideration. Make sure the moving parts are distinct from one another.

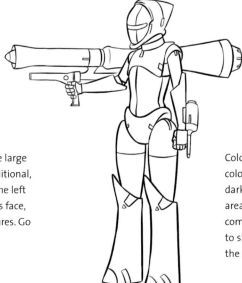

Develop the design of the large weapon and draw an additional, smaller piece as part of the left arm. Work on the mecha's face, giving him minimal features. Go over your work in ink.

Colour up your image. Apply flat colour to start with, adding darker tones to suggest shaded areas. Consider where the light is coming from and add highlights to show where it is reflected by the mecha's armour.

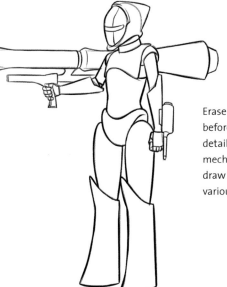

Erase any unwanted pencil lines before adding the last few details in ink. Consider how this mecha has been assembled and draw in hinges to show how his various parts move.

INDUSTRIAL MECHA

This mecha has been designed for a specific task in an industrial environment. It has bright lights for eyes and arms with pincer-like tools for hands, but no need for legs.

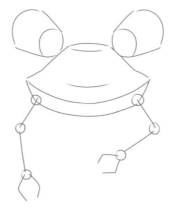

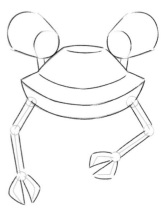

Start by drawing a very basic structure for your figure. This is a small, single, compact unit with two arms.

Add two geometric shapes for the light-beam 'eyes'. Draw in some small circles at the joints in the arms.

Use your basic structure to draw a fuller outline for your figure to make it look three-dimensional.

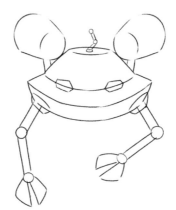

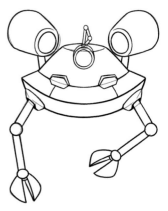

Make sure you are happy with the outline so far. Check perspective carefully and make any necessary adjustments.

Build on the detail, drawing hinges, sockets and joints. Start to draw the telescopic light attached to the mecha's top.

Go over your artwork in ink, refining your shapes. Draw in the telescopic light.

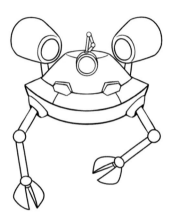

Erase any unwanted pencil lines before adding the finishing touches in ink.

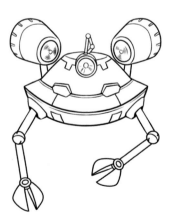

Finish the lights, adding a few lines to suggest the glass surfaces. Draw any seams in the metal and finish the joints.

Apply flat colour, using brass or steel shades for the working elements. Drop in some bright highlights where the harsh materials catch the light.

MEDICAL MECHA

The epitome of practicality, this mecha is small and airborne, which means she can get to the scene of an emergency in no time. She has a friendly face and colouring.

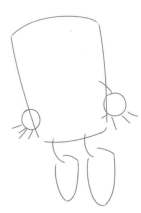

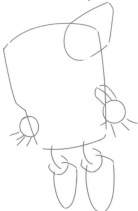

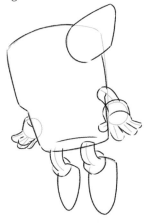

Start by drawing a very basic structure for your figure. This is a large, single unit with short arms and legs.

Shape the body a little and add geometric shapes for the hands and feet. Draw in the wing on the near side.

Work on the hands and feet. They are attached to tube-like flexible arms and legs. The hands have gloved fingers.

Make sure you are happy with the outline so far. Check perspective carefully and make any necessary adjustments.

Build on the detail, arm sockets and facial features. Work on the wing and draw in the backpack.

Go over your artwork in ink. Refine the shape of the near wing and add details to the shoes and backpack.

Erase any unwanted pencil lines before adding the finishing touches in ink.

Add the elements that make the mecha look factory-made: seams in the metal, screws in the feet, hinges. Add the first-aid symbols.

Apply flat colour, using a benign scheme. Drop in some highlights where the glossy metal finish catches the light.

GALLERY

You can develop every mecha imaginable, from evil-looking warriors to friendly automated pets. Think about colour choice and symbolism, both of which can be used to exaggerate a mecha's character or give it more purpose.

industrial mecha

below This mecha operates machinery. It has a single-unit body and rides on caterpillar tracks. It has strong, claw-like hands on arms that can rotate full circle.

flying eye

right This sinister little mecha is all about observation. It hovers in the air, recording all that goes on around it.

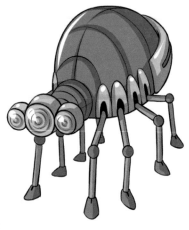

floppy bunny

right The inspiration for this mecha is part human part bunny. Despite being made of metal, she has a floppiness that makes her look harmless.

scary spider

above The outsize body of this spider is supported on eight double-jointed legs. The extended head makes the mecha look intimidating.

dummy

below This mecha has a comical body and a dopey look on his face. This gives him dumb personality and makes him a truly credible character.

mecha detector

right This mecha is rocket powered and needs no arms or legs. Its only device is a flexible tube with its weird detector.

security guard

right A solid looking mecha, with sturdy legs, thick head protection and huge, sweeping, bladelike arms.

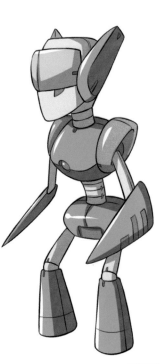

personal tv

left This handy little television mecha can follow you around to provide 24-hour entertainment. He can even change the channel by himself.

GALLERY

When developing mecha characters of your own, think very carefully about their functions and how they can influence appearance. Think about those features that might be more human-looking as well as those that are no longer necessary.

observation mecha

right This mecha has long, articulated legs that allow it to move freely above all else. It's function is purely to observe, so it has no need for arms.

all-seeing eye

left This mecha is, quite literally, an eye popped on top of a body. There is a comical aspect here, when you compare head size with skinny limb size.

domestic

left Scuttling around the house on the lookout for the occasional spill, this servile mecha keeps a dustpan and brush in his tummy-cupboard.

mecha dog

below This is a friendly companion that comes complete with happily wagging tail. It has a realistic form and proportions.

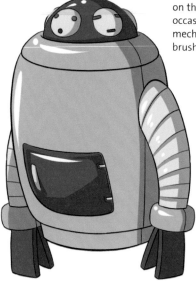

hovering mechanic

right This little mecha operates a machine in mid-air. He is small and compact and has no need for a more complex form.

superhero

above This is an alternative version of the medical mecha on pages 36–37.

scanning mecha

left Used as a scanning machine, this tiny desk-top mecha has sturdy legs for support, but no arms.

rocket giant

right This huge, solid mecha has strong articulated legs to support the weight and power of its rocket-launcher arms.

Chapter Three
Weapons: Fighting Manga

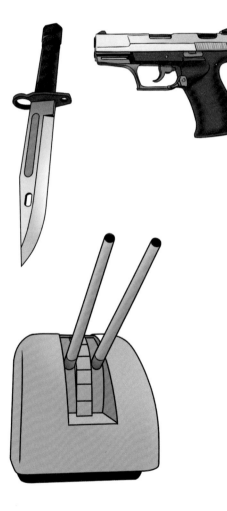

Many worlds exist in manga art, from the medieval forest, to intergalactic outpost. These places are populated by all manner of weird and wonderful characters. In this section of the book, you can discover the wide range of weapons that such characters might use, from a realistic revolver to a sci-fi-type laser gun. There is instructions for drawing a number of them, plus examples of pieces you might use for inspiration.

SWORD

This sword is based on the ancient Chinese dao, a weapon used for cutting and thrusting. It has a gentle curve from sword tip to hilt and a broad blade.

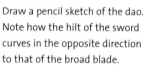

VARIATIONS

Draw a pencil sketch of the dao. Note how the hilt of the sword curves in the opposite direction to that of the broad blade.

Fine-tune your sketch, drawing the hilt in greater detail. This will help to make it look more three-dimensional.

Go over your drawing using ink, adding the slight bevel on the blade and wrinkles in the cloth. Erase unwanted pencil lines.

The sword is made from steel . Use high-contrast shading to capture its sheen. Use strong colours for the cloth on the hilt.

Look at pictures for inspiration. These are based on the Bowie knife, a short-handled dagger and samurai sword.

BOW AND ARROW

The simple bow and arrow was a popular choice of weapon in Europe and Asia during the Middle Ages. It is great for medieval, Robin Hood type stories.

VARIATIONS

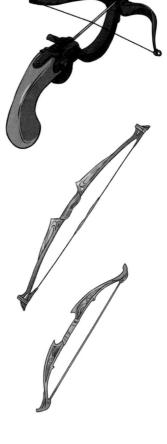

Begin by drawing a pencil sketch of the bow and arrow. Note the slender curves of the bow and the narrowness of the arrow.

Draw the bow grip in greater detail to make it look more three-dimensional.

Add detail. Draw in the cord grip on the bow and give the arrow shaft a tip and feathers. Go over your drawing in ink and erase any unwanted pencil lines.

Colour your work. The bow and the arrow shaft are made from wood. Use soft, warm browns. Emphasise the metal of the arrow with a couple highlights.

Alter your drawings to suit a storyline. You might want a crossbow instead, for example. Or use colour to tailor a design to a specific character.

GALLERY

Ancient worlds can be a fantastic source of inspiration when it comes to choosing weaponry for your manga characters. Whether defending their cities or on the attack, the ancients were incredibly resourceful makers of weapons.

dagger

below An effective stabbing weapon, this knife has a double-edged, tapered blade like those seen on similar weapons from ancient Rome.

brass knuckles

below Worn on the hand, brass knuckles have origins in pieces like the tekko, worn by the ancient Japanese.

side-handle baton

below These modern-day batons have origins in ancient Chinese nunchaku – two batons linked by a chain.

bo shuriken

below The ancient Japanese used lethal throwing blades, like these. They favoured them because they were easy to conceal for a surprise attack.

bow

above The bow and arrow is one of the most recognizable of all traditional weapons, and has an ancient history dating back as far as 8000BC.

bow and arrow

right With examples existing from Mongolia to medieval Britain and native America, there are countless bow types on which to base your own designs.

lethal blade

above Weapons like this were used in ancient Japan. They could be easily concealed in the palm before making an attack.

hira-shuriken

above This is a hand-held blade originating from medieval Japan. Pieces like this were used for throwing and stabbing.

yatagan sword

right This unusually shaped medieval Turkish sword has a long single-edge, forward curving blade.

Dao-type blade

below Based on ancient Chinese forms, this sword has a curved blade used for making sweeping attacks on an opponent.

medieval flail

above Swung above the head in a large circular movement, this nasty weapon has roots in the middle ages.

AUTOMATIC PISTOL

Handguns are great weapon choices for modern-day manga stories. Whether in the hands of a scheming criminal, a sinister spy or a professional law-enforcer, they are neat and easy to conceal. There is a brutal efficiency in their design.

Begin by drawing a pencil sketch of the pistol. Draw the weapon as a series of rectangles that you then give more shape to.

Make a more detailed sketch now. Refine the shape of the pistol. Draw in the trigger guard and surface details.

Go over your drawing using ink and erase any unwanted pencil lines. Draw any final details, such as the trigger and rivets.

VARIATIONS

Colour your weapon, paying close attention to materials. The dark steel of the gun should have sharp highlights where it catches the light.

Seek out references for other handheld weapons – revolvers, machine guns, and rifles are all great examples.

CANNON

When it comes to all-out war, why not opt for a heavy-duty artillery piece like this cannon? This is an early type, based on examples that might have been used during the Napoleonic Wars in Europe, or the American Civil War, both during the 19th century.

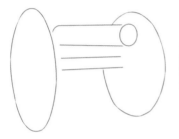 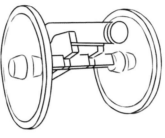 

Begin by drawing a pencil sketch of the cannon. Draw the weapon as a series of geometric shapes. Think about perspective.

Make a more detailed sketch now. Refine the shape of the cannon. Draw the wheels and axle in greater detail.

Give the wheels spokes and develop the gun. Go over your drawing using ink and erase any unwanted pencil lines.

VARIATIONS

Colour your cannon, using dull, military colours. Use darker tones for the shaded areas and use highlights sparingly.

Look around for other weapons with which to illustrate your stories – from futuristic rockets to realistic military pieces.

GALLERY

Many manga stories see one group of characters pitched in battle against another. They may be from different worlds and the weapons they use can be as diverse as a medieval bow and arrow to an alien laser and everything in between.

revolver

right The staple of film noir, the ladies' revolver. Small and compact, this weapons is easy to conceal before dealing that lethal shot.

alien phaser

below A handheld weapon that stuns the enemy using a light beam. Sometimes the victim completely disintegrates.

automatic pistol

left This efficient-looking weapon is a variation of the pistol shown on pages 48–49.

grenades

below Realistic-looking grenades in camouflage colours. These are quite often used for launching a surprise attack.

automatic weapon

right This sinister-looking weapon is the real tough guy's choice. The dark metal finish gives it a brutal appearance.

assault rifle

below This futuristic-looking weapon borrows elements from various guns, including the Russian AK47.

rocket missile

right This rocket is based on the French exocet, which was developed in the 1980s and designed for attacking warships.

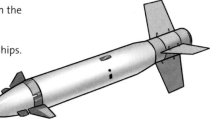

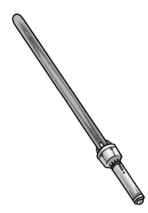

futuristic cannon

below This is a simple design, in keeping with the streamlined, paired back look that sums up our vision of the future.

torpedo

below A torpedo-shaped weapon, tapering towards the tail end. Fins at the mid-section and tail keep it stable in flight.

light sabre

above The mainstay of intergalactic battles, the trusty light sabre has a blade that can cut through almost any substance.

rocket launcher

below A powerful weapon with long-distance range, this rocket launcher is a staple of modern-day warfare scenes.

grenades

above Hand grenades based on the German WWII type, the long wooden handles enable the attacker to throw them considerable distances.

Chapter Four
Vehicles: Moving Manga

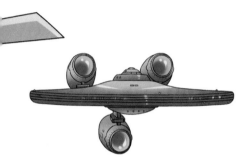

You can have great fun imagining scenarios in which vehicles might play a role – from a speedy getaway on a motorbike to a long-haul flight on a passenger jet. This section of the book looks at the various different types of vehicle that you might use to illustrate your manga stories and offers instruction on how to draw a handful of them. You'll also find suggestions for developing vehicle designs of your own.

BICYCLE

Although bicycles are notoriously difficult to draw, this version is seen side on – by far the easiest angle. The key lies in achieving the right proportions.

Using a pencil, draw a basic outline of the bicycle. Think about the proportions of wheels to frame.

Work on your outline to complete the frame of the bicycle and the wheels.

Use ink to blacken the tyres. This will help to make the bicycle look three-dimensional.

Work on the detail. Give the bicycle wheels spokes and draw in the pedals and bag rack.

Go over your drawing in ink, adding any last details such as the basket and brake cables.

Colour your work, using bright highlights where the metal frame catches the light.

MOTORBIKE

The principles for drawing a motorbike are very similar to those for drawing a bicycle. It simply has a larger, more solid frame. Sometimes, the engine is exposed.

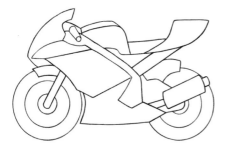

Using a pencil, sketch a basic outline of the motorbike using simple geometric shapes.

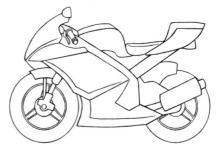

Work on your sketch to draw the motorbike in more detail, better defining some of the body parts.

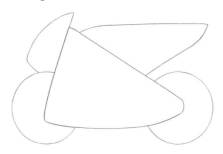

Continue to work on the outline. Draw the wheels and exhaust in more detail. Add the handlebars.

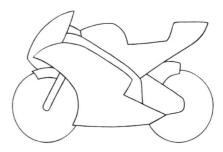

Add some finer details – the spokes in the wheels, the brakes on the handlebars, for example.

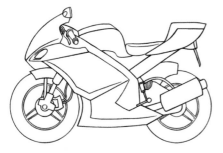

Go over your drawing in ink, adding any last details such as the rear light and brake cables.

Colour your work, using high contrast to show how the polished surfaces catch the light.

CAR

This sedan is seen from side on, so is a straightforward project. You can also base three-quarter view on this model – just consider perspective carefully when it comes to drawing the basic outline. The same principles can be applied to any model.

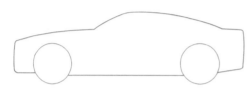 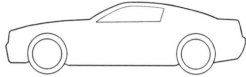

Use a pencil to sketch a rough outline of the car. Sketch the body of the car as a single unit and draw in the visible wheels.

Refine your basic outline, giving more shape to the front and rear profiles. Draw in the driver's window and the tires.

Use ink to blacken the tires. Draw in the wheel arches and give shape to the rear bumper. Start to mark the individual metal panels of the car.

Draw in some of the finer details: the wing mirror by the driver's window, the front and back lights, and the line of the hood.

Go over your finished artwork using ink and erase any unwanted pencil lines. Add any last details and finish the wheels.

Colour your artwork, using flat colour to start with. Add soft highlights to capture the gleam of the car and the reflective nature of its windows.

BUS

This is a large-scale American bus. Many European examples are modelled on this type. You can also look elsewhere for inspiration, designing models based on the old London double-decker, open-backed Routemaster or the super-long bendy buses seen in many of today's busy cities.

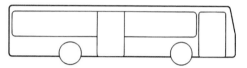

Using a pencil, draw a basic outline of the vehicle. This model is seen side on and is an almost perfect rectangle. Draw in the wheels.

Work on the outline, drawing in additional rectangles for the windows and doors. Thicken the outline over the top and to the rear of the bus.

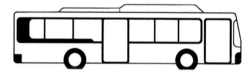

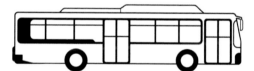

Use ink to blacken the tires. Still using ink, mark out the individual windows along the length of the bus. Give shape to the roof.

Now work on the details of the doors and draw in the rear view mirror to the front.

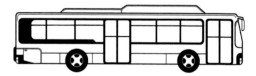

Go over the rest of your artwork using ink and erase any unwanted pencil lines. Finish the wheels and metal panelling.

Colour your artwork, using an appropriate colour. Lighten up the darker tones in places to keep the image looking three-dimensional.

BULLET TRAIN

This is a state-of-the-art passenger train, based on the Japanese model. It is seen from the three-quarter view, which makes the most of its aerodynamic design.

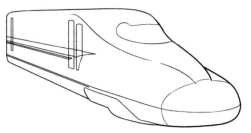

Draw a pencil outline of the train. Use a simple geometric shape to capture its sleek form.

Give shape to the engine section of the train to make it look three-dimensional.

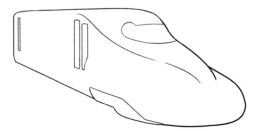

Give shape to the nose of the engine. Draw in the bubble window and the carriage doors.

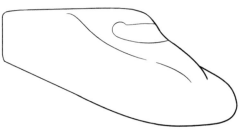

Work on the details: the striped logo down the side and the undercarriage of the train.

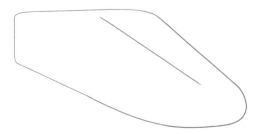

Draw in the windows. Go over your finished artwork using ink and erase any unwanted pencil lines.

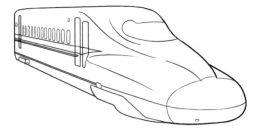

Colour your artwork, using appropriate colours. Add highlights to give the train a glossy, metallic finish.

AIRLINER

You can use the following model to draw an airplane of any size, from small-scale two-seater to Jumbo jet. This example is seen side on, so you need to think carefully about perspective.

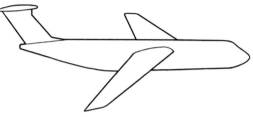

Draw a basic pencil outline of the plane. Use simple geometric shapes to capture its shape.

Give shape to the nose and tail sections to help make the plane look more three-dimensional.

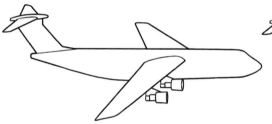

Continue to work on the tail section and draw the engines under the near wing.

Draw the wings in more detail, adding lines to suggest the movable flaps. Add the nose wheel.

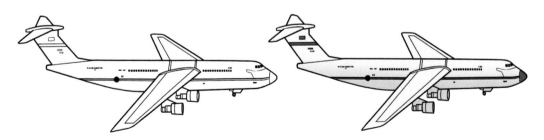

Draw in the windows. Go over your finished artwork using ink and erase any unwanted pencil lines.

Colour your artwork. Most commercial planes are white. Use subtle changes of light and dark.

YACHT

This is a luxury pleasure boat – the sort that you might see zipping along the coast in the south of France. It is seen side on, so perspective is important here. You can upscale this example to draw a cruise ship or passenger liner just as successfully.

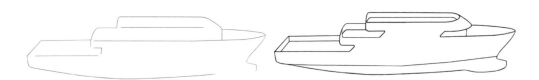

Draw a pencil outline of the yacht. Capture its basic shape at first, then work on the outline to sketch the body of the ship in greater detail.

Give shape to the bow of the yacht and mark out the individual decks to make your sketch look more three-dimensional.

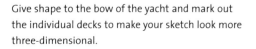
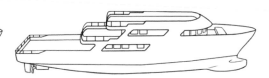

Mark out the rough layout of the windows that run the ship's length and draw in the railings around the deck edges. Consider scale carefully.

Finish your drawing by adding any final details, such as the windows to the front of the vessel and the propeller to the rear.

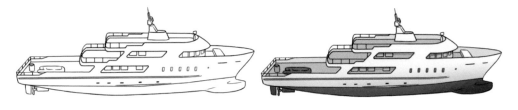

Go over your finished artwork using ink and erase any unwanted pencil lines. Draw in the remaining windows and the yacht's mast.

Colour your artwork. This vessel is predominantly white. Use subtle shades to suggest the contrast between light and shade.

SPACESHIP

You can use your imagination when it comes to designing spacecraft. This example is based on the Starship Enterprise from the Star Trek television series. Quite often UFOs tend to be flat and round, which is how they got the name 'flying saucers'

Using pencil, draw a basic outline of the spacecraft. This is, quite simply, a long, low, flat oval shape. Keep your lines simple.

Give more shape to your outline, to make it look three-dimensional. Start to add more structure at the centre, top and bottom.

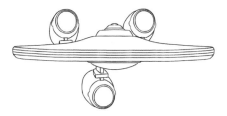

Refine the shape of the spacecraft at the top and bottom. Mark out lines across its width. These will eventually act as guides for the windows.

Draw in the three huge engines that are required for driving this craft forward. Now you begin to get a sense of the scale.

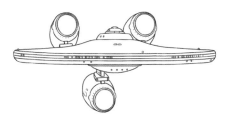

Now draw in windows, bearing the scale in mind. Go over your finished artwork using ink and erase any unwanted pencil lines.

Colour your artwork, using a uniform grey. Progress to darker shades in areas of shade and use bright highlights for contrast.

GALLERY

Here is just a small selection of the various vehicles that you can use to illustrate your manga stories. It is useful to consider a scenario in detail before adding vehicles, to make sure you have something appropriate and that suits the character who's driving it forward.

small car

right This two-door vehicle takes inspiration from the VW Beetle, and would suit a young, hip driver.

sedan

left This is a version of the car described on page 56, sporting a different colour scheme.

electric car

right A futuristic-looking, two-passenger electric scooter, suitable for driving busy streets in modern urban environments.

off-roader

left A hard-working vehicle with four-wheel drive – ideal for scenes with open terrain.

light aircraft

left This kind of airplane is the sort used by flying schools all around the world, and is a popular choice for amateur pilots.

superbike

right A modern-day, high-powered motorcycle – the sort that might be used for a fast getaway after a crime.

pedal bike

above A good old-fashioned pedal or bike, like the one demonstrated on page 54. It can be adapted to suit any rider.

jet bomber

below Based on the Stealth Bomber, this futuristic-looking supersonic aircraft will fly undetected over enemy airspace due to its unconventional shape.

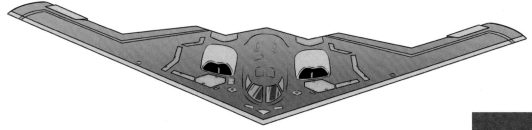

Chapter Five
Accessories: Dressing Up Manga

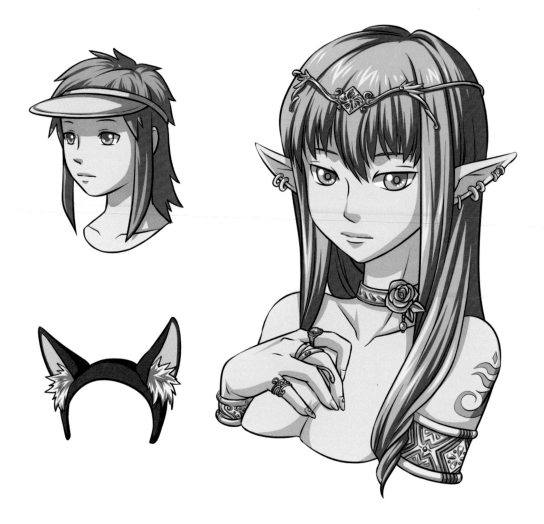

Quite often, a character will be made by his or her accessories – a disco diva and her plugged in headphones, the policeman and his whistle, the skateboarder and his bandanna. This section of the book offers a small selection of accessories, including hats, bags and scarves. There are step instructions for drawing a few of them, as well as advice on how to adapt almost any kind of accessory to suit the characters you want to create.

GALLERY

Accessories can be invaluable when it comes to giving a character personality, particularly once you start to develop stories around your creations. By giving your characters accessories, you make them stand out more from one another.

centurion's helmet

below Modelled on those of ancient Greece and Rome, this is a fantastic helmet with wing motif and visor.

knight's helmet

above Based on medieval versions of the knight's helmet, this is a simple design with useful visor.

dandy's hat

below A stylish and shapely felt hat with jewel and fur decoration. This could be worn by a male or female character and coloured accordingly.

gas mask

below Gas masks always have a sinister air to them. This could be adapted to create many other mask designs.

goggles

below Goggles offer a good accessory for a number of sports such as swimming, flying, skiing and motorcycling.

cat's ears

above A headband fashioned as a cat's ears, this is a great design for fancy-dress and can be adapted to suit any occasion.

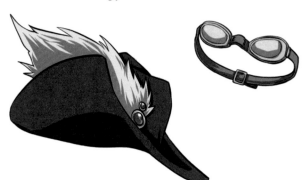

little bag

above This handbag might be suitable for ladies' eveningwear. It is small, compact and very easy to carry.

witch's hat

above All tattered and torn, this is the ultimate accessory for a gnarled old witch.

glasses

above Glasses are a surprisingly useful accessory. This model could be adapted endlessly.

day bag

above This is a design that could be drawn in any colour and with any motif. Its a great bag for everyday use.

backpack

above This design is in keeping with the sort seen used by European schoolchildren. It is both robust and practical.

beret

above This style of hat can be worn by girls and boys. You could also adapt it to serve as part of a uniform.

summer shade

above A girl's simple summer bonnet, with a bright ribbon and a pretty bow. It could form part of a school uniform.

bowler

right A jolly bowler in a custard colour and with a feather tucked into the hatband.

cross earring

below A simple enamelled cross attached to a hoop earring. This is the sort that might be worn singly by a teenage boy or girl.

neckerchief

above This is a design that can be worn by virtually any character and can be drawn to suit any style from hip-hop to punk to Wild West.

cat mask

above Masks are great accessories for manga characters, helping to conjure up an air of mystique. They can be benign or intimidating.

woolly scarf

above Easy to draw, the woolly scarf can be patterned or plain and may be worn by any kind of manga character.

workmen's gloves

above Gloves are useful for characters in winter outfits, but also suit a wide range of professions – firefighters, manual labourers, doctors.

plastic bangles

right Simple round bangles can be drawn in all colours and patterns. They can be studded with jewels and beads.

shell necklace

above A simple necklace with pretty shells threaded on a leather thong.

accessory An object or device not essential in itself but adding to the beauty, convenience, or effectiveness of something else; a thing of secondary importance.

ancient Of or relating to a remote period, to a time early in history, or to those living in such a period or time; of or relating to the historical period beginning with the earliest known civilizations and extending to the fall of the western Roman Empire in 476 CE; a person who lived in ancient times; the civilized people of antiquity.

bleed v. To ooze, run together, or spread beyond its proper boundary (as in ink); n. the part of a printed picture or design that overruns the margin.

ellipse A closed curve.

epitome A typical or ideal example; embodiment.

freehand Drawn or done by hand without the use of instruments or measurements.

gouache A pigment made of opaque colors ground in water and mixed with a preparation of gum.

graphic novel A narrative work in which the story is conveyed to the reader using sequential art in either an experimental design or in a traditional comics format. The term can apply to nonfiction works, thematically linked short stories, serial fiction, and long-form fiction.

humanoid Having human form or characteristics.

industrial Derived from human manufacture; used in or developed for use in industry.

inking Placing refined outlines over pencil lines using black ink and a pen, brush, or computer.

layout The manner in which something is arranged and/or illustrated, such as an advertisement, newspaper, book, or page.

malevolent Having, showing, or arising from intense often vicious ill will, spite, or hatred; productive of harm or evil.

manga Comics and print cartoons usually written in Japanese, published in Japan, and partaking of a Japanese style of illustration first developed in the late nineteenth century. Manga-inspired comics and graphic novels are now produced worldwide, but "manga" still generally refers to comics of Japanese origin.

medieval Of, relating to, or characteristic of the Middle Ages; having a quality associated with the Middle Ages; extremely outmoded or antiquated.

medium The singular of "media"; any material or technique used for the creation of art; a means of communication to the general public.

opaque Not letting light pass through; not transparent or translucent; not reflecting light; not shining or lustrous; dull or dark.

perspective The art of picturing objects or a scene in such a way as to show them as they appear to the eye with relative distance or depth; the appearance of objects or scenes as determined by their relative distance and positions.

pigment Coloring matter, usually in the form of an insoluble powder mixed with oil or water to make paints.

proportion Harmonious relation of parts to each other or to the whole; balance, symmetry; proper or equal share;

the relation of one part to another or to the whole with respect to magnitude, quantity, or degree; ratio.

sketch A simple, rough drawing or design, done rapidly and without much detail.

static Not moving or progressing; at rest; inactive; stationary.

variation The act or process of changing or modifying something without fundamentally altering its being or nature.

versatile Changing or fluctuating readily; embracing a variety of subjects, fields, or skills; turning with ease from one thing to another.

vibrant Throbbing with life and activity; lively; vigorous; energetic; radiant; sparkling; vivacious.

Comic-Con International
P.O. Box 128458
San Diego, CA 92112-8458
(619) 491-2475
Web site: http://www.comic-con.org
Comic-Con International is a nonprofit educational organiza-
    tion dedicated to creating awareness of, and appreciation
    for, comics and related popular art forms, primarily
    through the presentation of conventions and events that
    celebrate the historic and ongoing contribution of comics
    to art and culture.

Dark Horse Comics
10956 SE Main Street
Milwaukie, OR 97222
(503) 652-8815
Web site: http://www.darkhorse.com
Founded in 1986 by Mike Richardson, Dark Horse Comics
    has grown to become the third-largest comics publisher
    in the United States and is acclaimed internationally for
    the quality and diversity of its line and its ability to attract
    the top talent in the comics field. In conjunction with its
    sister company Dark Horse Entertainment, Dark Horse
    has over 350 properties, currently represented under
    the Dark Horse banner, serving as the jumping-off point
    for comics, books, films, television, electronic games,
    toys, and collectibles. Dark Horse distributes its charac-
    ters and concepts to more than fifty countries.

Del Rey Graphic Novels and Manga
Random House Publishing
1745 Broadway
New York, NY 10019
(212) 782-9000
Web site: http://graphic-novels-manga.suvudu.com
Del Rey Manga is a division of U.S. publisher Random House,
    working in conjunction with Kodansha, a leading Japanese
    manga publisher. With a primary focus on shojo and sho-
    nen manga titles, Del Rey Manga has established itself as
    the fourth-largest publisher of Japanese comics in English.

Fantagraphics Books
7563 Lake City Way NE
Seattle, WA 98115
(206) 524-1967
Web site: http://www.fantagraphics.com
Fantagraphics Books has been a leading proponent of com-
    ics as a legitimate form of art and literature since it began
    publishing the critical trade magazine the *Comics Journal*
    in 1976. By the early 1980s, Fantagraphics was at the
    forefront of the successful movement to establish comics
    as a medium as expressive and worthy as the more
    established popular arts of film, literature, and poetry.
    Fantagraphics has since gained an international reputation
    for its literate and innovative editorial standards and its
    superb production values. *Fantagraphics* was ranked
    among the top five most influential publishers in the

history of comics in a recent poll by an industry trade newspaper.

Kodansha International
Otowa YK Building 1-17-14
Otowa, Bunkyo-ku, Tokyo
Japan 112-8652
Web site: http://www.kodansha-intl.com
Kodansha is Japan's largest publisher, with its headquarters in Tokyo. Originally established in 1909 by Seiji Noma, the company is still a family-run business. Kodansha continues to play a dominant role in the media world, producing books and magazines in a wide variety of genres, including literature, fiction, nonfiction, children's, business, lifestyle, art, manga, fashion, and journalism. Recently, the company has ventured into digital distribution of content as well.

TOKYOPOP
Variety Building
5900 Wilshire Boulevard, 20th Floor
Los Angeles, CA 90036-5020
(323) 692-6700
Web site: http://www.tokyopop.com/manga
Founded in 1997 by media entrepreneur Stu Levy, TOKYOPOP established the market for manga in North America, introducing the term to the English language in the process. TOKYOPOP has published over three thousand books, distributed anime and Asian films on

home video and television, licensed merchandise to consumer goods companies, and created graphic novels of major brands such as Warcraft, Star Trek, SpongeBob SquarePants, and Hannah Montana. TOKYOPOP expanded internationally with offices in Europe and Japan and a network of over 160 partners in more than fifty countries and thirty languages.

VIZ Media, LLC
P.O. BOX 77010
San Francisco, CA 94107
Web site: http://www.viz.com
One of the first companies to publish Japanese manga for the U.S. market, VIZ Media publishes and distributes comics, graphic novels, novel-adaptations of manga, magazines, art books, and children's books. Based in San Francisco, VIZ also releases anime DVDs and handles licensing for its manga and animation properties.

Web Sites

Due to the changing nature of Internet links, Rosen Publishing has developed an online list of Web sites related to the subject of this book. This site is updated regularly. Please use this link to access the list:

http://www.rosenlinks.com/MAMA/Mecha

Amberlyn, J.C. *Drawing Manga Animals, Chibis, and Other Adorable Creatures.* New York, NY: Watson-Guptill, 2009.

Comickers Magazine. *Comickers Art: Tools and Techniques for Drawing Amazing Manga.* New York, NY: Harper Design, 2008.

Comickers Magazine. *Comickers Art 2: Create Amazing Manga Characters.* New York, NY: Collins Design, 2008.

Comickers Magazine. *Comickers Art 3: Write Amazing Manga Stories.* New York, NY: Harper Design, 2008.

Crilley, Mark. *Mastering Manga with Mark Crilley: 30 Drawing Lessons from the Creator of Akiko.* Cincinnati, OH: IMPACT Books, 2012.

Estudio Joso, ed. *The Monster Book of Manga: Draw Like the Experts.* New York, NY: Harper Design, 2006.

Flores, Irene. *Shojo Fashion Manga Art School: How to Draw Cool Looks and Characters.* Cincinnati, OH: IMPACT Books, 2009.

Hart, Christopher. *Manga for the Beginner: Everything You Need to Start Drawing Right Away!* New York, NY: Watson-Guptill, 2008.

Hart, Christopher. *Manga for the Beginner Chibis: Everything You Need to Start Drawing the Super-Cute Characters of Japanese Comics.* New York, NY: Watson-Guptill, 2010.

Hart, Christopher. *Manga for the Beginner Shoujo: Everything You Need to Start Drawing the Most Popular Style of Japanese Comics.* New York, NY: Watson-Guptill, 2010.

Hart, Christopher. *Manga Mania: Chibi and Furry Characters: How to Draw the Adorable Mini-Characters and Cool*

Cat-Girls of Japanese Comics. New York, NY: Watson-Guptill, 2006.

Hills, Doug. *Manga Studio for Dummies*. Hoboken, NJ: Wiley Publishing, 2008.

Ikari Studio, ed. *The Monster Book of Manga: Boys*. New York, NY: Harper Design, 2010.

Ikari Studio, ed. *The Monster Book of Manga: Fairies and Magical Creatures: Draw Like the Experts*. New York, NY: Harper Design, 2007.

Ikari Studio, ed. *The Monster Book of Manga: Girls*. New York, NY: Harper Design, 2008.

Okabayashi, Kensuke. *Manga for Dummies*. Hoboken, NJ: Wiley Publishing, 2007.

Takarai, Saori. *Manga Moods: 40 Faces and 80 Phrases*. Japanime Co. Ltd., 2006.

Thompson, Jason. *Manga: The Complete Guide*. New York, NY: Del Ray, 2007.

INDEX

About the Authors

Anna Southgate is an experienced writer and editor who has worked extensively for publishers of adult illustrated reference books. Her recent work has included art instruction books and providing the text for a series of six manga titles.

Yishan Li is a professional manga artist living in Edinburgh, Scotland. Her work has been published in the UK, United States, France, and Switzerland. She has published many books on manga, and she also draws a monthly strip, *The Adventures of CGI*, for *CosmoGirl!*